Twisted Path

Lisa Kathryn Jackson

Tellwell Talent
www.tellwell.ca

ISBN
978-0-2288-8903-8 (Hardcover)
978-0-2288-8902-1 (Paperback)
978-0-2288-8904-5 (eBook)

Table of Contents

Dedication

This book is dedicated to my oncologists:
Dr. Tam, Dr. McPherson, and Dr. Freeman.

This book is dedicated to my family.

This book is dedicated to my friends:
Maia, Brandie, Chelsea, Vicki, Nina, Lily,
Demi, Jasmine, Alisma, Glenn, Magnus,
Michael, Stephen, and my choir friends too.

Lastly, this book is dedicated to the patients I have met
during my time in the chemo clinics,
and to my friend Nathan.

Preface

This book has taken a total of ten-plus years to write, but the writing and sharing of my story process has been worthwhile. This book is not a medical journal, and I am not a medical professional. This is a combination of my patient experience as well as advice I've learned along the way, which I hope can help young adult cancer patients (and other cancer patients) navigate the system. This is an emotional look at my experience, details I wish I had known, and how much I've grown over the past ten years. As well, this is advice for medical professionals from a patient to advocate for others.

Acknowledgements

I want to thank my medical team for your guidance, help, and treatment. In Waterloo, thank you to Dr. Ismaili, Dr. Amy Tam, and Sue from Grand River Cancer Centre, as well as the amazing chemotherapy team, IR suite, and sixth-floor oncology teams. Out here in Victoria, thank you to BC Cancer Centre Victoria clinic team, Dr. Nicol McPherson and his team, Dr. Ashley Freeman and her team, chemotherapy suite nurses, and staff. As well, thank you to Dr. Clark, Dr. Flynn, Dr. Pathak, and the surgical unit at Royal Jubilee Hospital. I want to also say a huge thank you to my family for always being there and being so essential and supportive! Thank you to my work families, both Waterloo Heights in Waterloo and Amica Somerset. Finally, thank you to my friends Maia, Brandie, Chelsea, Demi, and Jasmine. Thank you to my D&D friends (Alisma, Glenn, Magnus, Michael, and Stephen), and to my awesome choir friends, The Choirs YYJ ☺

CHAPTER 1

Knowing something feels wrong

B ack in May 2012, in the morning of a busy day assisting residents with exercises and daily activities such as dressing themselves, I started to not feel well. I had been feeling tired and experiencing stomach pain over the past few months with repeated visits to the emergency department. I was given blood tests and sent home with at-home advice, with no success. At home advice included altering my diet, using a hot water bottle, and taking Tylenol to ease discomfort. I went home and made an appointment with my family doctor, who was quite kind about it. Knowing I was continuing to not feel well, my doctor booked me an appointment with a gastroenterologist. I thought, *Finally, I'll find out what is wrong. Is my age the reason why no one is taking me seriously?* I had a colonoscopy booked for the end of August. I was willing to wait to finally have answers. Based on the interactions I had with this gastroenterologist, I thought answers might happen.

Even though I continued to not feel well, the summer flew by. A feeling of relief came over me, knowing that something was happening and that I would finally know what was wrong.

The week of the colonoscopy was busy with prep, which was not enjoyable at all but worth it. I've heard prep is different wherever you live in Canada, and I was fortunate to have an easier prep, albeit uncomfortable at moments. August 25, 2012, arrived. This was a strange experience at my age. The first step was getting an IV into my arm, and after several tries, success! I walked into the room where the procedure would take place. I was instructed how to lie down and given the meds needed to fall asleep, or so I thought, and the procedure began. It was a strange out-of-body experience and I saw on the video screen the discomfort, the pain, the ache that my bowel was causing me. I saw the multiple spots in my bowel, and a blackened or ulcerated area too. I saw why I was feeling the way I did. Finally, I had the start of some answers!

The summer progressed. Fast-forward to October 3, 2012, and a day that would change my life for a few years, or many.

Advice from one patient to another:

Advocate for yourself.

- If you're not feeling well, talk to your doctor or emergency doctor and push for results.

- At the very least, request something over-the counter or an at-home remedy and if it does not resolve itself, then push for further tests.

This advice stems from not wanting to see anyone else have to wait to find answers. I wish that when I was in emerg, I had pushed to have a scan, or at the very least, an ultrasound, to rule out any major issues. The doctors ordered bloodwork and then gave me some over-the-counter medicines to help. So, listen to your body, if you feel comfortable, push for more testing.

CHAPTER 2

October 3, 2012

October 3, 2012! This day is etched in my brain forever. This was the day when I received a call from my family doctor, asking me to come in the office at the end of the day. He had news to share. I felt nervous, shocked, but also a sense of relief as I hung up the phone.

My mom and I entered the office. After a quick hello from his office administrator, we were ushered back to one of the examination rooms. My mom and I spent a few minutes in the room before my doctor entered and closed the door behind him. He was polite, professional, and not as jovial as he normally is. I knew something was wrong, but at the same time I was happy that I would have answers, finally. He cut right to the chase and shared the results of the biopsy during the colonoscopy and spoke in detailed medical terms. A few minutes later, he changed his tone and said, "non-Hodgkin's lymphoma, diffuse large b-cell lymphoma, and MALT lymphoma." *I have cancer at twenty-five years old*. I was speechless and couldn't think of what to say, but I felt grateful that my family doctor was the one to share the news. I was shocked and I had known something was wrong. I thought maybe colon cancer, but I never thought lymphoma. I was booked for an appointment, he mentioned, at Grand River Regional Cancer Centre on October 17, 2012, to meet my medical oncologist and begin the treatment process. I'm so glad that my mom was there with me. I did not want to hear the news alone. I thought, *I'm nervous but ready to begin the process. If I missed certain details of what was said, my mom can clarify for me, which is helpful.* There were moments of shock when hearing this news.

Advice for when hearing bad news:

- Have a friend or family member with you when hear your diagnosis or difficult news.
- If this is not a possible situation, ask for permission from your doctor to tape-record the conversation. I suggest this because you will not hear all the details the first time, no matter how much or how well you listen to your doctor.
- The other option is asking your doctor if you can take notes while your doctor is explaining your results. You can read these notes later and comprehend what the doctor said.
- When learning of this news, take time for yourself to comprehend the results or news as well as time for yourself for self-care.

- Self-care includes a good healthy meal, or a treat, also going for a walk – or run – in fresh air, reading a good book (one you enjoy), listening to music, spending time with friends and family.

CHAPTER 3

The journey begins

October 17, 2012, a day full of nerves but also, strangely enough, excitement or anticipation. I made the short fifteen-minute journey from my place with my parents to Grand River Cancer Centre. Once parked, stepping through the wooden doors, I knew this would be my second home for the next few months and I was ok with that, albeit nervous too. After checking in, which involved many questions and a screening form for symptoms to help the medical staff, we walked up the stairs to the clinic and were shown to a room to wait to meet my care team. This room was not the largest in size, but it was comfortable enough for my parents and the team. It was stark and sterile but somehow bright at the same time. I sat on the bed, nervously looking at the clock and chatting a little with my parents. A few moments later, a brunette middle-aged nurse with a bright welcoming smile came in the room and introduced herself as Sue, my supportive care nurse who worked with Dr. Tam. She opened her computer. Again, I shared my medical history. I knew this was a necessary part of the first appointment and completing the intake form so that the team could treat me well, both as a patient and as a person. Questions were asked, such as alcohol intake, medications, pregnancy, surgeries, and social questions as well about employment and culture. Prior to Sue leaving the room, I was given a bag full of resources to read post-appointment. These were mostly medical journals, information about how to treat symptoms and other important information. This was a little overwhelming to say the least.

Dr. Tam entered the room, followed by Sue, and I immediately felt very comfortable. Dr. Tam had a calmness, or a tactful yet professional approach to her demeanour. She introduced herself to me, acknowledged my parents, and then proceeded to open my chart. She closed it, made eye contact with me and spoke in layman's terms. She said that I was diagnosed with two types of non-Hodgkin's lymphoma (NHL), which were found in the colon. The one form is an aggressive form, diffuse large B-cell lymphoma, and a chronic form, MALT. During the week, I would undergo a round of testing to best tailor the treatment to my diagnosis. These tests would include a bone marrow biopsy, a gallium scan, and a CT scan. Despite how nervous I felt for the tests, I felt a sense of comfort and in good hands with this team.

My parents and I left. I was somehow ready for this diagnosis but couldn't help but also feel a little numb. This would be my life for the next few months. I was just truly happy for answers and had finally obtained them. I spoke with my manager at Waterloo Heights and shared this news. They said that my job would be held for me until I returned, which was a relief to hear.

I returned to the cancer centre two days later, bright and early for a bone marrow biopsy. Entering the chemo suite, I sensed a calm bright open space full of nurses and other staff who really love what they do. I was ushered to the back of the suite into a room where they perform procedures such as blood transfusions and bone marrow biopsies. I was greeted by a kind nurse who made me feel at ease despite how nervous I was. The nurse prepped me for the procedure. I was given a medication into the upper part of my arm which eased my nerves a little. Dr. Tam entered the room, and I was grateful it was her performing the procedure with her familiar calming voice. I was able to have my mom in the room and she was a great support. I lay on my back; freezing was injected in my right hip, and the procedure was performed. A biopsy was taken, and I was able to stay in the room and rest for about ten minutes which was a plus. While resting, Shirley, one of the centre's volunteers, came into the room. She offered a warm blanket and some very helpful information while navigating this centre. I felt a sense of comfort and ease and focused on that.

I had a few hours before the CT scan and decided to purchase some water. I couldn't eat before the CT scan. As a distraction, we decided to walk around the hospital and check out the common areas. We spent most of the time in the gift shop, which was very well stocked. We spent time window shopping, but nothing worth purchasing caught our eye.

Looking at our watches, we thought it was worth heading to the CT scan so I could begin my prep. I would give myself time to drink the icky contrast solution. I walked in the CT suite and was greeted by a kind CT technician who gave me the solution in a large Styrofoam cup to be completed prior to the test. I was also encouraged to have my hospital gown on early so I could leisurely enjoy the solution. While enjoying this lovely beverage, my mom, with magazine in hand, and I were sitting across from a middle-aged gentleman dressed in a hospital gown himself. He did not realize he was wearing a hospital gown and his posture was quite the sight! Fortunately, this vision was short-lived as he was called into the room shortly after.

A few minutes later, I was called into a separate room to be given an IV to help with the test. The tech attempted to start the IV but due to my lucky history with veins, they needed to have a member of the IV team assist with obtaining a vein. I was frustrated with myself but also realized it was not entirely my fault. My deep and rolling veins would quickly meet many medical team members in this hospital. A fifty-year-old female nurse entered the room and was able to obtain my vein on the first try which was reassuring and eased the nerves.

The CT scan was rather quick, and I got changed into regular clothes and left the hospital. I would be heading to another hospital the following day for a gallium scan.

What I remember from a gallium scan is that it is like a CT scan but an IV did not have to be obtained. This was great news to my ears. I just had to be injected with a reactive iodine which meant I could not travel for a month without having a medical letter in hand stating why there was this solution in my system.

The following week, on October 24, 2012, I made the trek to the centre with my parents to hear the next steps and any results. This appointment was mainly Dr. Tam discussing my treatment. I would begin treatment the following week on October 30 with a full slate of chemotherapy in the suite as an outpatient. I would not begin right away, due to the nature of the location of my lymphoma and the strength or toxicity of the chemo and the risk of bowel perforation. So, for a week, I would start part of my chemo, which was prednisone or the P in R-CHOP. The dosage was 100 mg per day for a week, and then I would continue this for five days after chemo. I was pleased to begin part of my chemo and ready yet a little nervous for side effects.

During this week, my brother visited. I cut my hair short in a pixie cut, which would hopefully make eventually losing my hair a little easier. I enjoyed maybe a little reprieve prior to the next set of medications.

On October 30, 2012, first day of chemo, I entered the centre, completed my every-visit intake, and made my way up to the chemo suite. I was greeted by a very kind nurse who ushered me to my chair for the day. The chemo suite at the centre has beautiful big windows and nice comfortable chairs. I wore very comfortable clothes and settled into my chair starting about 9 a.m. Little did I know that a long day was ahead for me.

One of the senior nurses on staff started my IV. Pharmacy patient teaching occurred, and I started my medication plan with one small hiccup. I started

Rituximab, and approximately one minute into treatment I started feeling flushed and my throat was bugging me. My mom, who was sitting beside me, said I looked red, and the nursing team jumped quickly into action resolving my allergic reaction before it worsened. I was given Benadryl and a steroid, and the treatment of this medication was slowed down. There were no other reactions, and we proceeded to the other medications that were planned for the day. While treatment proceeded, I spoke with several kind people who made the day as enjoyable as possible. My mom bought me a sandwich and tea from Tim Hortons, as I couldn't leave the suite. I also enjoyed some salt and vinegar chips, which were helpful with the nausea. I had taken two anti-nausea pills pre-treatment which helped as well.

I completed the day with my mom and I being the last two people in the centre, along with the care staff. I was told that being done at six forty-five p.m. was normal, which was reassuring. When I got home, I had a bit of an appetite and enjoyed some quiche for dinner. I was told one of the symptoms of treatment is nausea and vomiting, and like clockwork, a few hours after treatment, I experienced those symptoms. I went to sleep soon after and the next day, I was fortunate to not feel too bad. However, two weeks later…

Advice for patients when meeting oncologist:

- The first time meeting your doctor can be scary but there may also be a feeling of relief, which is normal. These feelings are normal and natural – do not feel strange for having them.
- Bring a supportive person with you a spouse, a parent, a child, or a friend. This person should be willing to listen to the oncologist, and maybe be a note-taker if the oncologist allows.
- From my experience, you do not hear or might hear incorrectly what the oncologist says regarding diagnosis or treatment. The other person in the room with you allows you to have the chance after the appointment to debrief and clear up any details that may not have been heard correctly.
- Post-appointment, stick to reading through any resources that the oncologist or nurse has given you during the appointment – do not google or search the internet for information because you may come across information that is not correct.

When a friend, family member, or coworker has been diagnosed with cancer, it might be hard to know what to say or what not to say. These are not rules; they are from my experience of what has been appreciated or what I wish someone had not said.

What to say to someone just diagnosed with cancer:

- *I'm sorry.*

    o   When there is nothing else to really say or you don't know entirely what to say, this is so helpful. "I'm sorry this happened to you...but I'm here."

- *Any favourite foods? Can I bring you something?*

    o   Meal trains have been so helpful for me during chemo. Sometimes the side effects, whether it's the fatigue or the nausea, cause meals to become a challenge. You don't know what you want to eat, or the taste of food is not there due to medication, or your energy level is not there.

o From my experience, always accept food or treats that are made – it's someone's way of helping.

o Ask if there are types of foods such as spicy or gluten or lactose that your friend or family member cannot have before bringing food to them.

- *Can I help with groceries or watch a movie with you?*

  o These are concrete ways of helping your friend or family member or coworker who has been diagnosed. Maybe they want to be alone and do not want help or company, but at the very least, you've offered, which is appreciated.

  o When diagnosed there is a sense of control or normalcy that is lost, so when friends offer their help or company, it feels like the normalcy of self is still there.

- *Send a message, send a text, call them.*

  o This is so that the person knows they're not alone or at least that the friend, family member, or coworker is checking in to see how they are doing.

- *Give them a hug.*

    o   This is a controversial topic during lingering COVID, but a hug is needed. The best is when someone doesn't know what to say but gives their friend, family member, or coworker a hug; it is so comforting.

On the other hand, there are phrases and statements that should not be said to someone diagnosed with cancer, going through testing to determine treatment, or going through treatment. There may be many more phrases or statements, but I will outline a few that I have heard. Avoid making these statements.

What not to say to someone just diagnosed with cancer:

- *You don't look sick.*

    o   What am I supposed to look like? During my very first rounds of chemo, when I lost my hair and eyebrows, I looked sick or like the typical patient. However, during the more recent chemo treatments, I have not lost my hair, but I still experience side effects.

o   Please do not say this…especially to someone with an illness you cannot see. I know it may mean that the person looks healthy, or that you are trying to be supportive. An alternative phrase could be "I'm glad to see you today. I'm glad you're here. It's good to see you."

- *Nothing.*

  o   When someone tells you they've been diagnosed, they tell you this because they trust you, they feel comfortable enough with the news to share, and they care about you enough to tell you. If you're not sure what to say and say nothing but give the person a hug, that is totally ok (from my experience). It may be because you're still processing the news yourself and are not sure what to say but want to be supportive, so a hug is your way of being supportive for your friend, family member, etc.

However, if someone shares with you their diagnosis and you say nothing, saying nothing makes the person wonder why they shared the news in the first place.

- Everything happens for a reason.

    o   Instead, you could say, "I'm here for you; I wanted to let you know I care…" Basically, say anything but this phrase.

- Be happy you got the good cancer.

    o   There is no good cancer.
    o   There are cancers with harsher treatments than other cancers, but there is no good cancer to be diagnosed with.
    o   Just don't say this…ever!

- What doesn't kill you makes you stronger.

    o   As much as I love this Kelly Clarkson song, I hate this phrase.
    o   As a patient you find resilience, strength, or whatever positive feeling you need to get through the treatment plan in front of you. The chemo and radiation are harsh but necessary treatments. These are necessary to destroy the cancer cells. However, there are side effects of chemo which may lead to a hospital visit due to an infection.
    o   Just please don't say this…There's not a good positive alternative for this phrase.

> • As much as possible, try not to treat the person as an ill person. Try to include them in activities as much as possible. At least extend the invitation, and they can decide whether they feel up to attending.

If an activity, gathering or event people who might have, a cold or the fluit would be risky for the person to attend, especially at their l

It is cool, helpful, and appreciated to find media that is relatable to a situation you are going through. There are cancer survivors who have created comics, cards, and other forms of media online that share the truth behind how survivors and patients are feeling.

As a survivor, I know that friends and family and coworkers are trying to process the news about the person's diagnosis and experience, and these are just some helpful tips to hopefully make that conversation easier.

Once you complete any necessary testing prior to treatment as deemed by your oncologist, you will be scheduled for your first chemotherapy treatment. Note: I will not mention any details about radiation treatment because I did not experience any radiation treatment during any of my diagnoses.

The first day of chemotherapy is understandably a daunting one, but here is some advice to help:

- Arrive at the centre early, in plenty of time.
- Arrive with a supportive person to accompany you for the day (during COVID this may not be the case but have a person available to drive you home post-treatment).
- Bring your health card and medications (if needed, such as anti-nausea).
- There might be instructions from your team to take your medication before you arrive or when you arrive (a certain period time before treatment).

  o Follow these instructions – this will be extremely helpful during your treatment and in the hours post-treatment as well.

- Arrive in comfortable clothes.

  o My favourite was fleece jogging pants and a T-shirt with a hoodie (the chemo suite was cold).
  o If you have a Port-a-Cath, wear a button-down shirt or a shirt or a tank top that can have the port easily accessible for the nurses to access and place a dressing over top of it for the duration of your treatment.

- The nurses in the chemotherapy clinic are incredible; you are in great hands. You are in a very supportive environment and will be well taken care of regarding safe delivery of medication, bedside manner, and care during your treatment.
- Bring water and tea, snacks, and lunch for the day (depending on what amenities your centre has). My favourite snack is always salt and vinegar chips. They are very helpful and easy to digest during treatment.
- Bring a laptop, novel, knitting – anything to keep occupied.
- Bring a blanket if you have one that is your favourite from home, and you will likely be offered a warm blanket from someone in the centre/clinic.

  o Take these ☺. With some of your treatments, they may be helpful.

- Ask your nurses if you need help or if any symptoms develop.
- Bring a notebook just in case to take notes, especially if you have a pharmacy patient teaching during your first treatment.

o   You will likely be advised to go to your centre if this occurs. After hours, you might be advised to go to the nearest hospital (please refer to the information provided to you).

- You may also be given information regarding your medication and whether it is covered by your health plan.

    o   Staff will help with medication coverage. They will send you in the right direction for other community resources if they are unable to help.

- If you have any questions during your treatment day, ask. The clerks, nurses, and other staff are happy to help.

    o   They want to make sure you're as comfortable as possible or at least have the resources you need prior to leaving as well as knowing who to contact if you have any issues prior to your next treatment.

CHAPTER 4

Two Weeks Later

Two weeks later...

I woke up on November 11, 2012, and my scalp started itching and hurting. I took my temperature, as advised by nursing staff, and it was 38.3 degrees. I did not feel well; I felt flushed and feverish. I proceeded to get dressed, and then my mom and I made the drive to the cancer centre. We arrived and noticed the centre was closed due to Remembrance Day and decided to proceed to the emergency department. I entered the emergency department, went through triage, and was immediately sent to the "chemo" or isolation area. This is the area of the emergency department to keep immune-comprised patients safe from other patients prior to a bed opening in the department. I did not sit in this area for long and within minutes was escorted to a bed in the department. I was greeted by a nurse who proceeded to take my vitals, draw blood, and then leave the room. I sat in the room with my mom for two hours without an update, but I was glad my mom was there because I was able to sleep a little bit and try to keep distracted. Two hours later, another nurse arrived in the room and proceeded to tell my mom and me that I would be admitted to the inpatient oncology unit.

Arriving on the floor, my first impression was that it was very stark, sterile, and comforting yet slightly scary. For the first time since my diagnosis, I felt like I was in hospital. I was trying to stay positive. I was escorted to a private room with a TV and phone, which made the hospital stay a little more comfortable. Aside from speaking to and being treated by the nurses, I wanted to sleep. My temperature was taken again, and it was 39 degrees. I felt flushed and was given saline through my IV to cool down my body temperature. It was eight p.m., and I was left alone for a few hours to sleep. At four a.m., my temperature was taken again, and it was 39 degrees. I guess the chemo worked well! I woke up at seven a.m. to a kind day shift nurse who gave me an antibiotic to feel a little more human. Accompanied by the hospitalist, the nurse told me that my ANC count or absolute neutrophil count was 0.5 which required hospitalization and meant I had no immunity. I was started on the antibiotic and given a medication injected into my stomach called Neupogen which would raise my ANC.

When the nurse and hospitalist left, I realized that I had been too distracted to notice that, well, on my pillow was a large amount of my hair. The fact that my scalp had felt itchy and painful the day before meant I was losing my hair. I was warned about this, but I wasn't truly prepared for how strange and shocking it felt. There was still some hair on my head, but it didn't look great.

My mom combed it for me. As this was happening, the hospital phone rang; it was my dad calling from Ottawa. He was in Ottawa for a few days helping take care of my grandpa who had taken a turn for the worse. He had called to check in.

That night after dinner, my mom and I had a visit with a hospital volunteer dressed as a clown who visited patients on the unit. He wheeled a TV into my room with a VHS and a box of movies. He was a welcomed visitor after the day I had. In the box was a VHS of an old Backstreet Boys concert. I had watched this video more times than I can count but proceeded to pick it out of the box and play it once the volunteer left the room. I decided to focus on something fun that I could control despite how cheesy it was; I didn't care.

The next morning, bloodwork was drawn at approximately five a.m. and then the hospitalist visited a few hours later to check in, continue the antibiotic, and inform my mom and I that the Neupogen was working. My ANC count had increased from 0.5 to 2.1, which was a great improvement and meant I could go home. I was filled with emotions but also relieved to be discharged. I had a prescription for the antibiotic, a prescription for the Neupogen, and a note in hand to proceed to CCAC office (or home care) to learn how to inject the Neupogen myself into my stomach muscle.

After being discharged, I went to the pharmacy, and they filled the order for the Neupogen, or Grastofil, and an antibiotic; and this is where I learned about the cost of the Neupogen. This life-saving medication is worth 250 dollars a vial (or a one-time injection). My parents covered the cost of this medication. We made the drive out to CCAC, and I learned how to inject myself intramuscularly, which was needed so that a home nurse did not have to do this for me.

This hospital visit was very enlightening for me, and traumatic and terrifying. It was an experience I needed to have. I knew the chemo was working, so that was a positive moment, along with the volunteer that I met.

Tips for unexpected hospital visit:

Some chemotherapy treatments have a risk of neutropenia, or a risk of infection, especially during the low point in treatment. The low point in treatment is the time when your counts are the lowest, typically day ten to fourteen of your treatment cycle, however, you will be advised of these times while speaking with your oncologist and chemo nurses. During your first chemotherapy treatment, you will be given a letter and a paper. The letter is for the emergency nurse and doctor, and the paper is for you. The paper tells you to call the nursing line if you experience certain side effects. As well, the paper advises you to seek emergency attention if you experience certain side effects such as a fever. Fever temperature is 38 degrees Celsius or higher.

During the day ten-to-fourteen period, especially, but at any time during your treatment, if your temperature reaches the fever temperature, you head to your closest emergency department and present this letter. If you start to feel unwell before reaching the fever temperature, pack a bag, just in case, with a book, a change of clothes, a toothbrush, toothpaste and a charger. Your family member or friend could bring this too. The feeling of heading to the emergency department may be nerve-racking or stressful, and so having this bag ready takes some of the stress away. The nurses and doctor are extremely helpful and have a wonderful bedside manner. They will complete any necessary procedures like bloodwork in the department, and they will have a treatment plan for you to help you feel better and resolve the temperature.

While in hospital, talk to your medical team and the nurses in charge of your care regarding any dietary needs you may have, such as, vegan, vegetarian, celiac, lactose intolerance or others. Allergies should be addressed as well. They will do their best to accommodate these dietary needs, while communicating with Nutrition and Food Services.

CHAPTER 5

Losing hair

As I shared in the previous chapter, my head started feeling itchy, red, and sore. I had been warned that I could potentially lose my hair with the treatment I was being given. The reality was hard when I woke up that morning with hair on my pillow. I had already cut my hair short, and so there wasn't much to lose. But the fact that half of it was on my pillow, in the hospital, was a hard moment. In that moment I realized I was a patient; this would be my life for many more months, or potentially years. My mom made a joke that she could film shaving it, or film my hair the way it was. Her joking helped and made me laugh. I, for some reason, have become a fan of dark humour…not sure why?

When I was discharged from the hospital and had my first shower at home, more of my hair fell out. At this point I knew I had to shave it, but I didn't feel comfortable doing so. I wasn't going to have my parents shave it. So, I went to a local hair salon, but not my usual salon. I went to a salon where I didn't know anyone, where a lovely gentleman, who had experience with wig-fitting and cancer patients, shaved my head. Once my head was shaved, it felt freeing: my new reality. He also fitted me for a lovely human hair wig, which I took home with me that day. I tried on it again, a day after it was fitted. I had very sensitive skin, which ended up not feeling very comfortable underneath the wig. I kept the wig, but my head pieces ended up being toques and cotton caps, and while spending time at home, I walked around the house with my bald head in full view. I didn't care. I fortunately didn't feel cold not wearing a cap or a wig. I felt more comfortable once the hair loss experience was complete. Again, I felt in control of something. As I was losing my hair I didn't feel in control; I felt cancer was taking something away from me, part of my sense of identity. However, once the experience was complete, and I could walk around with no hair or wearing a toque, I felt better, more like me. It's hard to explain, but it became easier to accept.

Advice from my experience of losing my hair:

- Cut your hair short if your hair is not already short.
- If you know you will likely lose your hair, have a wig already purchased, or toques/caps – whichever you will feel more comfortable wearing.

- If you are not shaving your head yourself, have a friend, a family member, or perhaps a hair stylist you feel comfortable with shave your head.

The feelings you are feeling while losing your hair are completely normal and real. It's ok to cry, it's ok to be angry, it's ok to feel whatever you are feeling.

CHAPTER 6

Port-a-Cath

An early December morning came rather quickly. The nerves were present, but the opportunity to have an easier time at chemo made the nerves diminish a bit. This procedure was unknown, but I had confidence in the doctors, nurses, and staff performing this procedure.

My mom and I made the short trip over to Grand River and were met with the admitting nurse in the outpatient surgery area. After vitals and discussion of the procedure, I was given an Ativan. As I started showing how nervous I was, one of the nurses reassured me she'd be in the room with me, which somehow convinced me to continue proceeding toward the interventional radiology suite. In this suite, they use fine instruments and a machine to help the doctor or surgeon perform this and other procedures.

The Port-a-Cath procedure was necessary; I guess it could have been worse. Let's say it's a necessary evil, one to have only if you do not have great veins. I am someone who does not have great veins, so I decided this was the best decision for me before proceeding with remaining treatments. If you want to save yourself from the pre-chemo anxiety of IV access, then definitely do this procedure.

I was sent home later in the day with plastic and tape running from the bottom of my chin to just below where the Port-a-Cath was inserted, which was near my jugular vein in my upper chest muscle. The next day, CCAC or home care sent a nurse to clean the area where the Port-a-Cath was inserted to prevent infection and then apply a new bandage. However, a short time after she left, I started feeling itchy redness under the bandage. My mom was home with me and noticed this itchy redness. I called my supportive care nurse at the centre. She advised removal of bandage.

I was given medication from the centre to relieve this blister bandage, and fortunately the Port-a-Cath was free of infection and able to work properly for my next treatment. A different bandage would be used during treatment.

Advice regarding Port-a-Cath:

- Each hospital and centre is different.
    - o Some centres will flush your port prior to chemo so you will not have to worry about the timing and maintenance of your port.

o   Some centres will require you to have your port maintained (or flushed) between treatments via community care (or home care nurse).

- Follow this guideline carefully because it will help to maintain the health of your port.

CHAPTER 7

Dealing with hard times during chemo and finishing chemo

For my first time back in the centre since the Port-a-Cath had been inserted, I knew I'd be in for an easier treatment, but with having this new device in my chest, I wasn't sure what to expect. The anxious feelings I had felt while the nurses tried to access my vein went away. During this time, not only was my family dealing with a family member in the midst of chemo and fighting this disease, but my dad also lost his dad. My dad spent time in Ottawa while his dad was passing away and for the funeral. At the same time, my mom lost her sister to ovarian cancer. The emotions that surfaced from losing two family members within a short period of time were hard. I'm not sure if these emotions were from the guilt for not seeing my grandpa, or from wishing I had spent more time with my aunt, or perhaps from my parents having that additional news to process on top of my own feelings. I guess being in chemo was something to focus on.

I did manage to get to my aunt's funeral. She lived a few hours away from me by car, so travel was easy. I walked into the funeral home in Owen Sound and was immediately greeted by staff who worked at the home. One of them said that they had heard about my health from immediate family (my uncle and cousins) at the visitation the night before. When walking into the home, the first interaction with the staff felt awkward. Maybe I was brave…maybe it was good that I came to the funeral. I continued farther into the home and saw other family members including my cousins (my aunt's kids). I chatted for a bit and felt comfortable and more at ease. I came in wearing a mask because of my strong treatments. I needed to stay healthy. I came to say goodbye to my aunt, and to say thank you. *Thank you for your strength while you were fighting. Thank you for your sense of humour. Thank you for taking each day, no matter how hard they were, day by day, or "It is what it is."* This is the reason I came to the funeral, also to see my uncle and my aunt's kids.

The funeral finished and we had some time to chat and eat in the next room. Some of the interactions between family members were awkward, and tension filled the air. When we decided to drive back home, I was ready to go.

A few weeks later, my dad attended the funeral for his dad in Ottawa. I had not seen my grandpa for a few months and there was a bit of guilt for not attending but it was safer for me not to go to the funeral.

Christmas passed, and we celebrated a new year: 2013 and the finishing of my main treatment. I knew I would be continuing one of my medications to help keep the lymphoma at bay. It was targeted or immunotherapy, and a plan for "maintenance" would be determined once I finished this main treatment. In February 2013, I completed six rounds of chemo. No more bald head, no more fatigue, no more loss of taste or having most foods except scalloped potatoes taste like metal. I needed to celebrate, or at least have a small victory of getting through these rounds with all of the strength I could muster.

Dealing with the end of chemo – or main chemo:

For some cancers like lymphoma, you will have a treatment schedule of four to eight cycles depending on your chemo protocol. Then, you will be told about maintenance treatment. I was told that maintenance treatment is to continue to fight against the cells that produce the indolent or slow-growing or chronic lymphoma. The goal is to have the lymphoma not return for a long period of time, hopefully forever. So, chemo continues. Hair will return. Energy may return slowly. It will return and you will recover, but take the time to rest if needed.

I am not well versed in any other cancers, so I can't speak about other patients I've talked to and their experience. I can say that some patients will be done after their last main chemo treatment, and some may have more treatment. It is best to check with your oncologist for your specific protocol or plan.

What I will say is that no matter what your protocol is post-main chemotherapy, it is important to celebrate! Celebrate making it through these rounds of chemo, celebrate the end of side effects, celebrate the amount of strength it took to deal with the physical and maybe emotional side effects too. You deserve to celebrate this part! I celebrated by having lunch out with family friends from our gym.

CHAPTER 8

Start of immunotherapy and emotions that surface

I took a few weeks off after my main chemo to recover my energy before heading back to work. I told my manager that I would need a day off every few months for this maintenance treatment but otherwise I was back at work. I was still wearing my toque or cap because my hair was just starting to return. The residents were happy to see me and knew what I was dealing with. They told me to take my cap off and were interested in seeing the progression of my hair returning.

At the beginning of May, 2013, I had my first day of immunotherapy or Rituximab in the clinic. I sat again on the infamous chair. I was in for a much shorter experience but an intriguing one, nonetheless. I had a lovely nurse administering this medication which was not available until 2005. Prior to this medication being administered, I was given hydrocortisone and another med to prevent an allergic reaction.

I brought a magazine to keep myself entertained while this medication flowed through my veins. Fortunately, I did not feel too many side effects from this – well, aside from tiredness and a lower blood pressure. This was a new experience for me. I felt more like myself physically, but at the same time, emotions surfaced. I saw patients in the clinic who were resilient in their strength, managing to deal with effects while enduring some harsh chemo. I felt strange being in the clinic while feeling more like myself and having my hair, albeit short, but still: I had my hair.

There is one experience I will not forget because it reminds me to never say this to anyone – not that I would, but it still reminds me. There was a support person in the clinic with her family member who came back after getting a coffee at Tim Horton's. As she walked past me, she stared at me and said, "You don't look sick."

There were many things I wanted to say to her, but I let it go. Cancer comes in many forms, and just because I don't look like the stereotype of the typical patient with the bald head, weight loss, and what you "normally" see, I'm still dealing with this.

This protocol was one round every three months for two years, so I could and did work during this time. When the final round approached, I couldn't wait; I was also nervous subconsciously. Maybe the nerves came from fearing reoccurrence, or maybe it was from being finished with this plan or protocol and getting my energy back enough to work full-time again. Nonetheless, January 21, 2015, arrived, and I was excited. The premeds were given (I had taken some at home), and the bag of Rituximab was hung from the IV pole. I didn't tell many people that I was dealing with this event, experience, moment… so the reaction when we posted about my final day of treatment was expected. The support and comments of congratulations were very much welcomed.

My IV was taken out, the medication was completed, and I went to the spot in the clinic reserved for the traditional ringing of the bell. I grabbed the bottom of the bell with my hands and started ringing it. A multitude of emotions surfaced, and I started crying. I felt relief, joy, nervous, excited…the list continues but I tried to focus on the positive emotions of the day, no matter how nervous I was. We had a lovely celebration at a local restaurant with a few people from our gym.

Two weeks later, I was back to work fully. My coworkers and the residents were happy to see me back. It was back to the usual return of meal service, happy hour, and other activities, but I had a new appreciation for everything and everyone. *Maybe this is what I should focus on: the little things.*

Advice during immunotherapy treatment:

- Every person and their reaction to treatment is different. There are side effects of the immunotherapy you are being given.

---

o   For me, Rituximab caused my blood
pressure to drop, but safely to a
manageable level. The fatigue remained
but decreased over time. I had an
allergic reaction to treatment initially,
so I was given premeds to prevent this
reaction. My duration of treatment
was also lengthened to help with the
prevention of a reaction.

•   But no matter the treatment or the side
effects, my best advice is to listen to your
body.

o   If this means returning to work while
undergoing immunotherapy treatment
– do this.

o   If you have the option to take time off
while you recover – do this.

CHAPTER 9

Living as a survivor and losing someone

After treatment I was experiencing my "new normal" of appreciating the little things and trying to focus on hobbies, exercise, and creative outlets. I focused on these hobbies and creative outlets because I was now out of the world – the world of a patient – that I had been in for three years. As a young adult, this was a period of my life where I should have been doing the typical things, such as working at a career job, maybe getting married, buying a house, moving to a new city. Instead, I was sitting in the chemo clinic recliner, attached to my IV pole, being given meds that would save my life and prevent this cancer from returning for a long period of time, hopefully for good. These three years involved countless bloodwork draws, doctor visits, needle pokes for IVs or my Port-a-Cath, which was eventually removed due to not needing it anymore. It was hard to finally focus and shift my attention to being back in the real world: the world of visits to the grocery store, work, movies, or other activities and hobbies. This is why my focus on creative outlets, hobbies, and the gym were so important, as they reminded me of who I really am.

I looked forward to the visits to our local gym and seeing the members who I and my mom had connected with before and during my treatment days.

My rehearsals with the choir I was involved with were even more appreciated than before. I joined this choir as I was going through maintenance treatment. Before joining this choir, I had not sung in a choir since high school. I always listened to music and sang during treatment. I looked forward to each rehearsal and the music we were preparing for our upcoming concert.

I also focused on the positive parts about my work, and my appreciation for the residents. I enjoyed working with my coworkers and making the residents' days a bit more enjoyable, and I also became more involved with some of the activities as well. These activities included happy hour, talent shows, and our annual fashion show. These were enjoyable activities to focus on, but they were also treatment away from the fear of reoccurrence, the fear of being back in the centre. I didn't fear being back there. I knew I could handle it, because I had already managed to make it through three years of my life. I needed a distraction, especially during the first few months. Maybe it was just that: a life-changing experience and being back there. I couldn't wrap my head around that being an aspect of my life again. I was seeing friends getting married and having kids while not asking me how I was doing. Perhaps that is why I used activities at work, music, and the gym as distractions. These feelings became less and less over time, or I have been able to manage them better over time. As well, my check-ins with my oncologist on a three-month or six-month basis helped as well. They were the reassurance I may have needed.

During treatment, you may meet other patients that you connect well with or develop a strong connection or friendship with. This happened to me. I joined a young adult cancer support group in Kitchener and connected with an awesome group of people. One of the people was Nathan, who had been out of chemo for leukemia for the past month. He was a fellow survivor. He was in remission. I was NED, or no evidence of disease. We went for dinner, participated in fun activities together, and enjoyed our time together. We enjoyed the fact that we could experience our new normal doing regular activities out in the community but also chat with each other about all of our experiences during treatment. As well, we could share how we were feeling too.

He shared that his leukemia had returned. Perhaps I was trying to help, or to just be there for Nathan as he was going through treatment. He unfortunately had a really hard time with treatment. We met for lunch one day. I didn't know this would be the last day I would see him.

Advice for living as a survivor (from a survivor's perspective):

- Once you ring the bell during your last treatment, you have finished your treatment protocol, or your main treatment protocol. You may have feelings or different emotions which arise to the surface; this is normal.

  o However, in the days and weeks to come, if you feel like you need to talk to someone aside from your friends or family, do so. It is ok to seek help for any emotions you are experiencing.
  o If there is a local counsellor, or outpatient psychology or psychiatry – reach out to your oncologist to see if they have any recommendations of someone to speak to.

- Find an outlet, whether it be creative or going to the gym, or go for a run (if cleared by your doctor).

  o This outlet will be a distraction or a fun experience outside of the patient world.

- Lean on your friends or your family, and if you need support regarding side effects post-chemo, or with groceries and cooking, ask for help.

- Your days and weeks to come post-chemo or post-radiation may be joyful or really hard. These feelings are ok – you have been through a life-changing experience.
- If there is a scan after your treatment, do not worry (if possible).

    o   You can't change your results.
    o   Go for a walk. Listen to your favourite music.
    o   Watch your favourite show. Go for a coffee.

CHAPTER 10

New move, new centre, new oncologist

My parents and I discussed moving, and we figured out our new spot to live. We decided that moving out West, to Victoria, BC from Kitchener, was our best next life move. July 28, 2016, came and the cars were shipped out. We brought our suitcases and boarded a plane: first to Calgary, then en route to Victoria. Our plane arrived late in Victoria, and after staying the night in Sidney, we made our way to our new place in Victoria, near the harbour, which was pretty and a much-needed view. I made the adjustment to living in a completely new city for the first time in my life. I'm very glad I made the move to the same city as my parents, closer to my brother and sister-in-law. I knew it was time for a change, so it was a good change.

My chart made the move as well, from Grand River Cancer to BC Cancer. I had my first appointment with my new oncologist in September 2016. I walked into the beautiful centre in Victoria, located on the Royal Jubilee property and was impressed. I felt very comfortable as I walked in, and I knew I had made the right move. My mom was with me in the waiting area on the second floor of the centre, and then we were taken back to the appointment room by a patient care aide. The difference between centres is that I was expecting to see a nurse, or a supportive care nurse, alongside the oncologist, but this was not the case. I waited in the room, and a lovely Scottish gentleman walked in and introduced himself. "Dr. McPherson," he said. He was a researcher of lymphoma and breast cancer, so I knew I was in good hands. I had a longer appointment with him. He assessed my past treatment and stated that he would see me every six months or so. I had also filled out a questionnaire before seeing Dr. McPherson, so he and the centre had up-to-date information regarding my symptoms, my health history, and how I was feeling.

As I left the appointment, my mom and I walked around the centre. We noticed the gift shop, the library, the bloodwork area, the pharmacy, and the chemo suite. I'm glad I made the move, both for personal reasons and regarding my medical care as well. I appreciated the bedside manner, tone, and approachability of Dr. Tam, but I was now appreciating being assigned a caring, extremely knowledgeable oncologist. When you know the date of your move to a new town and your first appointment with a new oncologist, speak to your current oncologist and the administration staff to begin the transition process of sending your chart to the new centre you will be attending for your treatment. Confirm with new centre that they have received your paperwork and your chart.

CHAPTER 11

Something is wrong, again...

I had just spoken with Dr. McPherson in April 2017, and then I woke up a month later and noticed a huge lump on my neck. I knew it would likely be a quicker diagnosis, but I was, at the same time, nervous and a little scared of the reoccurrence. I immediately called the centre and talked to Dr. McPherson about next steps regarding this lump. I was pleasantly surprised at the speed in which I was booked for a biopsy – a core needle biopsy in particular.

I arrived at Jubilee Hospital a week after I saw the lump and spoke with Dr. McPherson. The staff in the diagnostic and treatment centre were kind, professional, and very caring while I had this procedure. The doctor performing this procedure outlined what to expect. Then, the doctor froze my neck and used a long needle to sample some of the lymph node in my neck. I received a call a week later that they hadn't retrieved enough sample to make a diagnosis, and so I was booked to see an ENT to surgically remove a portion of the lymph node in my neck. The doctor I spoke to, Dr. Pathak, was incredible. His bedside manner, professionalism, and clarity when explaining this procedure gave me a lot of confidence that this biopsy would work. He managed to book a spot for me rather quickly at Jubilee to complete this procedure.

Two weeks after this procedure, I went to see Dr. McPherson. I was told that my aggressive lymphoma had a less than five per cent chance of returning but my chronic or indolent or slow-growing lymphoma had returned, and it was in my neck. I would receive a call to schedule a date for treatment. I was full of emotions. I was appreciative of how quickly my diagnosis was achieved. I was shocked that I was back in this world, but I was ready to fight. I would be starting a treatment including Bendamustine and Rituximab. Rituximab is a drug I was familiar with.

Prior to starting chemo in July, my mom and I travelled to Vancouver where I underwent a PET scan at Vancouver's BC Cancer Centre. I could not say enough positive remarks regarding the staff at Vancouver's BC Cancer Centre. Everyone's emotions during a diagnosis will be different. However, my best advice is to remember that the doctors are there for you, and your oncologist is there for you. Based on the biopsy, scans, and blood tests, they will determine the best course of treatment for you. Ask any and all questions you have. Do not google; Google is not your best friend. This is from experience. If you can have someone with you during this period of time to support you, it is really helpful.

CHAPTER 12

Gratitude for medical team and starting chemo (again!)

In July 2017, chemo began again...
I entered a brightly-lit chemo clinic on the second floor of the centre. I was greeted by a lovely nurse, who, with her experience, managed to get my IV started on the first try. I sat in a comfy recliner, as comfortable as these chairs can be. I was in a chair that had a view of the room. I was given some paperwork, similar to what I had received in Ontario. I was given a paper instructing me to call the nurses' line or go to emergency if I experienced certain side effects. I was also given a letter to give to the emergency doctor if needed. The nurse started the Bendamustine, and my mom grabbed a warm blanket to wrap around my arm because the Bendamustine can potentially sting in the veins. I was warned about this side effect. At the same time, saline was given. Later in the morning, I finished the Bendamustine and then started the Rituximab. Prior to starting the Rituximab, I was given Tylenol and Benadryl. This was a change from my experience in Ontario, where I was not given premeds prior to my Rituximab.

The nurse started the Rituximab at a low rate to see how I tolerated it. At every duration, I was asked how I was doing and if I felt any sort of allergic reaction. Fortunately, I did not experience an allergic reaction this time. It was a long day, but fortunately I did not feel any adverse effects.

I was fortunate to have a great nurse, and I felt very comfortable in the chemo suite with any of the nurses who were checking on me. This treatment occurred every three weeks for six rounds. The lump decreased in size during treatment. Partway through maintenance treatment, I was told that Rituximab would now be administered in the form of an injection, not IV.

This was welcomed news to me, given the fact that I do not have the best veins. Due to family history, or genetics, I'm blessed with deep and rolling veins, or reactive veins as one of the nurses mentioned. I was grateful to not have as many side effects with just Rituximab as I had experienced with Bendamustine and Rituximab. I could work while having this maintenance treatment, which added a bit of normalcy. I even started singing with a local choir while finishing this maintenance treatment. My two takeaways from these new rounds of chemo and being diagnosed again is that no matter what province you're in, the nursing team is incredible and you're in great hands. It is a hard process, but you will find the feelings or strength or grit you need to handle it. Chemo does damage to the veins, and if you have deep veins (like me), there is extra gratitude toward the nursing team when they manage to get a vein. A port was not needed this time around.

CHAPTER 13

The Choirs YYJ

I took a break from the world of choirs when I moved out West in 2016. In 2017, I began looking at local choirs in town, and The Choirs always came to mind, especially when watching their YouTube videos. I started with The Chorus (part of The Choirs) in February 2019 and felt a great connection to this music-loving pop folk community. They are an amazing group of people. I proceeded to join in on The Choirs' summer shows, such as Beacon Hill and Butchart Gardens. This was all while continuing with the immunotherapy (or Rituximab). I continued with The Choirs as we joined West My Friend for their anniversary concert show, which was such a fun experience. I switched to The Choir after West My Friend due to a change in work schedule. I had been warned that this was a rowdy group, but I was ready for it.

In terms of my experience and life as a patient and survivor, I didn't share this right away with the Chorus (when I first started) or with The Choir. I decided it best for them to get to know me first: the quirky sense of humour music-loving me. The me who tried D&D years ago, decided to jump back into it, and love it… me. I decided to approach my incredible director (and friend) Marc via email and ask if it would be ok to sing for the choir buddies post break. He said absolutely, and I proceeded to sing, with accompaniment from Erin, on piano "You will be found" from *Dear Evan Hansen* for The Choir buddies that evening. Once I finished singing this, Marc broke the ice and asked me why I chose this song, and I proceeded to share that I had been dealing with lymphoma and was finishing chemo the day after that rehearsal. I was not entirely sure how the choir buddies would react, but the sound and support from them was unlike anything else; they were so supportive, and it was so special!! I sang "You will be found" because I found that they saw me, and I could be myself in this group and be accepted, which was great. A few days later, we celebrated post-chemo at Ten Commons.

This celebration weekend started with watching our director's gig at a local venue along with the choir buddies. The next day, we celebrated at Ten Commons. I ran a few errands prior to the evening. I headed to Ten Commons and thought I would be early, but I wasn't. We enjoyed a fun evening together over food and drink. In the busy establishment, I made an awkward speech, saying how strong and genuine everyone was and how much I appreciate their support. Moments after I sat down, my friend Michael spoke, and the main words I remember from his speech were that I had spoken about how strong they all are, and he said how strong I am, and everyone agreed, which made me cry, but a happy cry. I am still singing with this group to this day, and playing D&D with some of them, and I could not be more grateful.

There is no real "advice" for this chapter.

From patient to patient, if you can find a group of friends who share the same hobby as you and accept you for you, especially during treatment, do it.

CHAPTER 14

The theatre kid in me…

In a previous chapter I spoke about finding a creative outlet for yourself, whether it be painting, running, singing, or others. A creative outlet helps, whether as a distraction or to allow you to focus on who you are, not the patient you may feel you are. For me, aside from choir and my music, it is a game called Dungeons and Dragons. In late 2019, a friend of mine ran a one-night game with a few friends from choir to see if there was interest and just for fun too. An email was sent a few weeks later with questions about our character, creating said character, and giving our friend, the DM or Dungeon Master, said details. We showed up on a Thursday night, in James Bay, with character details, character sheet in hand, or ideas about our character in mind, not knowing what to expect. I left that evening pleasantly surprised by how much fun I had.

I had not told the group what was going on with me; I just wanted to learn, enjoy, and have fun playing this game with some great people. I enjoyed delving into and figuring out the traits of this fiery elf named Clara who was more quiet, secretive perhaps, just finding her way in the world. The week before I shared with my choir, I shared with this group what was going on with me. With finishing treatment, I was able to be myself. The "theatre kid in me" was able to shine through. Like Clara, I gained the confidence to find myself too, away from the patient world. This shift was due to not having to think about what I was going through. Instead, I could appreciate the friends who were at the table with me. They delved deeply into their characters, showing me that I could rebuild my confidence by playing this character. We explored other stories but always came back to this story, and it was (and is) memorable.

Fast-forward to March 2020, and my first thought was, *What will happen to this group, being told "no evidence of disease," living with this lymphoma, and isolating away from friends?* Fortunately, members of our group knew of technology we could use, like Discord and Roll20 (and Foundry), and we continued meeting weekly. This was much needed within our group as we dealt with our emotions and frustrations throughout this pandemic. We continued to play throughout the pandemic, exploring characters within the stories and checking in with each other. In September 2021, we started playing together in person again, and it was such a wonderful feeling. I had missed seeing everyone in person, checking in and getting that boost that the game provides.

We continued to play in person, but while we played, I didn't feel right. I felt drained of energy, stressed, similar to how I felt prior to being diagnosed in 2012.

As much as I shared, I didn't want to share the entire round of testing with everyone including how nervous I was about lymphoma. No matter what I shared, they were so supportive and maintained the teasing, fun, and challenging nature of the sessions. We even began a new campaign in 2021, with a new DM from our group at the helm. A grittier, gothic horror campaign, which was a welcomed distraction and an enjoyable challenge. This campaign allowed our DM who organized the initial campaign to be able to play which was great as well.

I wanted to write a chapter in this book both about the players and DM, and about D&D, this math rocks improv game I love so much. This game is a bit of an escape. You can play a character who perhaps has personality traits you want to explore about yourself, or a character who is far away from who you are normally. This game has challenging rules, but it is great for the brain. Most importantly, I want to talk about the people. The game is wonderful, but it's only wonderful if you have friends at the table you trust. You must be willing to improv or roleplay to collaborate in creating a memorable story with exciting combat and interesting conversations. I'm lucky to have found that with this group!

Finding a hobby which you love and enjoy exploring with an element of fulfillment is important. Such hobbies are important because they allow you to explore outside of yourself and find what you've always wanted to do.

If there is something that you've always wanted to do, be open to trying it. If you can try a hobby with friends, do this. Be open to getting to know the people who are part of this hobby; you might find an awesome group of friends.

CHAPTER 15

Something is wrong…again!

A year after I finished treatment, I started experiencing a persistent cough that wouldn't go away. I spoke with my oncologist. I underwent a scan, which found nothing of concern. About six months later, I was connected with a different oncologist, Dr. Freeman, for a short time, who requested some tests to determine what was happening. There were no definitive results. In the months to come, I experienced weight loss, night sweats, fatigue, and a persistent cough.

In July 2022, I called my oncologist's secretary to mention that I had been experiencing these symptoms. Within two weeks, I underwent a CT scan and a bronchoscopy courtesy of Dr. Clark, a pulmonologist. She had an incredible bedside manner, and I felt very comfortable with her performing this biopsy.

She called me on July 22 with results about why I had been experiencing these symptoms the past several months: I had indolent or low-grade lymphoma in my lungs. I had cancer, for the third time. This was hard, especially hard, because it required new grit, new strength, new…

I was fortunately able to sing with my choir the next day at Beacon Hill Park. This much-needed experience with my friends was a welcomed distraction. The support shown by my D&D friends and choir friends was incredible and made the news much easier to deal with. I could continue to be myself around them, which has meant the world.

I started chemo on August 16, 2022, and this was one of the hardest days since I was first diagnosed back in 2012. It's hard to pinpoint the exact feelings of why it was one of the hardest days. One reason is that the cancer is in my lungs, making it harder to sing. Another reason is being back with the same nurses, being back in the chemo world, and being back to feeling like a patient.

The part of my life that has really helped, aside from having the time off work, to rest, heal, laugh, enjoy nature and gain my strength back is my family and friends (choir friends and work friends). I have been fortunate to have the energy to participate in special events and attend rehearsals. My friends are very conscious of my situation. We wear masks at choir and stay home if we feel any cold, flu, or COVID symptoms. I am very fortunate to have a supportive community of family and friends while going through my current rounds of chemotherapy.

I share my current situation within this book because I hope it can perhaps be relatable to someone reading this. I am sharing both what has happened in the past and what is happening currently to me, so that a patient reading this knows they're not alone.

Conclusion

This is my story, one I am willing to share because I want to offer insight into my experience to potentially help others going through the same or a similar experience. When I was diagnosed, there weren't many, if any, resources for a young adult going through cancer. There were no real, honest resources sharing advice and experiences that I could find relatable. There were many medical journals and medical professionals around to answer any medical-related questions like side effects, but there wasn't a book, a journal, that outlines a relatable experience.

Thank you for reading this book. I hope that my experience and my advice from this life-changing experience provides help to someone or to a family member or friend looking for advice about what someone special in their life is going through.

For caregivers or support people, my best advice is to listen to your friend or family member going through this experience and remember that they are still the same person, even with no hair, even with nausea, even while sitting in the recliner chair or going to various appointments. Another piece of advice for the caregiver or support person is to take time for yourself. As much as you are there for the person, you have to be there for yourself too. Rest, food, and watching your favourite show are just as important for you as well. As well, if you are a friend of the person going through treatment, always try to check in with them, and invite them to events. They may not want to go to the event, but that is their decision. Let it be their decision.

For the patient, any feelings you are experiencing may be a normal experience during treatment. If there is a support group in your community, this may be a helpful place for you to express these feelings. Perhaps chatting to your family member or friend might be helpful. From my experience, music, drama, or art may be helpful as well. The gym, if it's ok with your oncologist, might be an option. Find the positive creative or physical outlet to help you through this experience.

From one patient to another, I do not know how you are feeling or what medication you have been prescribed prior to chemotherapy and during chemotherapy. However, I can tell you that you will make it through this, or if the cancer is more advanced, you will manage your side effects the best you can with help from your team. The patients I have met are the most incredible people. I have not met you, but I believe that you are an incredible, inspiring person who is in great hands with the team at your centre. Read your favourite book, watch your favourite show on repeat, and eat your favourite food. If you need to lean on your friends at times and tell them how you are feeling, do that.

Manufactured by Amazon.ca
Acheson, AB

10970059R00042